– A Small Hotel in Cornwall –

The Lobster Pot
of Mousehole

Diana Ayres

Illustrations by Daphne Radenhurst   Original captions by Kate Tilley

This edition of
A Small Hotel in Cornwall: The Lobster Pot of Mousehole
is published in 2008 by

Trungle Books
Trungle Vineries
Paul, Penzance
Cornwall TR19 6UG

ISBN 978-0-9559482-0-6

Book design by Donna J. Anton

Printed in the United Kingdom
by Rowe the Printers
Hayle, Cornwall TR27 4PZ

*I*n the long history of Mousehole there was, for a short period, a small hotel and restaurant that attracted visitors from all over the world.

If you mention this tiny Cornish fishing village almost anywhere, more often than not someone suddenly will break into a nostalgic smile and say, "Ah! I remember the Lobster Pot."

It is because of affectionate memories like these, enhanced by Daphne Radenhurst's enchanting artwork, that this little book was written.

Diana Ayres
June 2008

The story of the Lobster Pot really began in 1947, when Major John Kelly took on the challenge of turning what was then a small café, with a very uninspiring décor, into a hotel.

In all the years since then, nothing has better captured the Lobster Pot's quirkiness and charms than the following illustrations by Daphne Radenhurst accompanied by Kate Tilley's captivating captions.

For one enchanted summer, in 1952, both women worked there together. Daphne was the receptionist – and the glamorous red-haired Kate, the manageress.

Kate's brother was the film star Kenneth More, who at the time was shooting "Genevieve," the box-office hit about the London-to-Brighton vintage car rally. Kate's own exuberant personality lent an atmosphere of sophisticated fun to the place.

Once upon a time, on a very grey day in London,

I longed to be far away.

I remembered Mousehole – pronounced Mowzel – with its fishermen leaning, always leaning, against their favourite buildings,

and the washing hanging round the houses,

and a small hotel I visited once when I was young and very
happy.

So I wrote a letter to the owners of the small hotel which was called "The Lobster Pot" and asked them for a job. They gave me one, and in March I became the Manageress.

*B*ut the real stars of the Lobster Pot back then were the owners – the enigmatic Major Kelly and his delightful wife, Cinders. It was their vision, charm and excellent manners that placed it head and shoulders above ordinary hotels.

Its location, moreover, was breathtaking. The veranda, then open to the four winds, overlooked the harbour and Mounts Bay beyond.

*A*fter taking over, Major Kelly, with great gusto and a good deal of willing help from friends from Sheffield University, who spent their holidays in Mousehole, set about converting the building. In fact, so many of his chums offered a hand they had to be accommodated all over the village. This enthusiasm helped to earn the hotel and restaurant its international reputation.

Major Kelly and Cinders had style, and it showed. They had an old grey Alvis and on sunny afternoons the kitchen staff would pack them a hamper. Cinders would tie on a delicate headscarf, place the basket in the back of the open-top car along with their beloved Golden Retriever, and the Kellys would motor off for a picnic in the stunning Cornish countryside. Other times they visited Branscombe, in Devon, where they had a house called "Cobblers."

Not only did the guests adore the atmosphere of the hotel but the staff fell under its charm as well. Each day the Major gathered everyone together to learn what their day was like and if there were any complaints. He taught them how to pour wine and to treat the guests graciously, including buying the daily papers to make their stay as pleasant as possible.

It was a time before anyone was sent to "catering college," so the staff under the Major's guidance did their own "eccentric thing," and the customers loved it.

Most memorable for the staff were the wonderful meals they shared at the end of shifts. Like the generous host he was, Major Kelly sat everyone around a big table for plenty of fun and laughter.

I come to Mousehole

My life in Mousehole began. First I had to pass the "leaning" fishermen – who were "some" fussy.

Then I had to please my staff. There was Sylvia, Gwen and Nita in the dining room.

The cook and her helpers in the very small kitchen, which seemed full of people all looking for a place to do things!

Mrs Kneebone, Barbara and Noreen did the bedrooms, lounge
and generally helped elsewhere.

By the 1950's the Lobster Pot's cuisine was already building a fine reputation, with a menu ahead of its time.

After a drink in the cocktail bar guests could dine on lobster, of course, plus locally caught crab, Angels on Horseback, eggs Benedict, and a firm favourite with many local families, Tournedos Rossini – fillet steak, fried bread and pâté with a Madeira mushroom sauce.

So sought-after were the restaurant's recipes for Lobster Thermidor and Lobster Pot Crab au Gratin that they were featured in a national women's magazine in 1966.

Staff and guests mixed together. It was a time when customers expected the staff to have a drink or cigarette with them. Major Kelly bought rounds and staff and guests would reciprocate. No nanny state in those days!

The hotel was more like a country house – customers and staff jelled like an extended family.

Everyone wanted to chat with Cinders and Major Kelly, who often took the late sitting in the restaurant. He had a fount of amusing stories and his charm kept the guests entertained well into the night. Business was brisk, and the restaurant served over 100 covers nightly.

Such was the popularity of the hotel that further accommodation had to be found in cottages around the village. Some of these lacked the latest in "mod cons," but they proved popular – and many visitors chose to stay in them on return visits.

One local cottage owner was asked to be a witness at the wedding of an American guest who had stayed with her whilst making up her mind whether to enter into matrimony. The wedding took place at Paul church, and by way of thanks the Mousehole woman was given a bracelet as a memento. Her daughter wears it to this day.

But it was not *all* hard work. One afternoon, when business was slack, the waiters took the opportunity of doing a little fishing from the balcony into the harbour below. Their luck was in and they landed a five-pound mullet – served up later to the guests, of course.

People came from all parts of the world to this small hotel.

They were greeted by Major and Mrs John Kelly . . . "Mandy,"
a nice bitch . . . her son, "Henry" . . . "Suzie" and her kittens
. . . and "John Willie," who had great character and sharp
claws.

Mayor & Mrs. Kelly, the proprietors, with Maude and Henry, Suzy, Ellen Wilby & the kittens, and various local inhabitants

He played Hamlet once

Major Kelly once played "Hamlet,"

and Mrs Kelly did splendid things with flowers.

Even before the Lobster Pot came into existence the building had seen exciting times. None more so than when it was used for the wedding celebrations of the poet Dylan Thomas and his bride, Caitlin.

After tying the knot at Penzance Register Office they returned to Mousehole. There was much merriment and music. However, whilst dancing with a local fisherman, Caitlin's wedding ring slipped off and fell to the ground. The two were found by Dylan crawling around the feet of the dancers, since losing the ring was considered a bad omen. Luckily, the ring was later found.

Another early visitor was Agatha Christie, who set a murder mystery in the village – and called it Rathole.

And in 1938, almost 10 years before Major Kelly took over the property, the "wickedest man in the world" paid a visit. Aleister Crowley, also known as the Black Magician, is said to have spent a holiday there. By all accounts he enjoyed a plain and wholesome time – sunbathing, walking, rock climbing and taking photographs. The charm of the place must have worked on him. It was just as well, since he was also a friend of author Ian Fleming's, and it has been suggested that Crowley's persona was the basis for all the evil villains in the James Bond stories.

Mousehole was very different just after the war. It was the early days of tourism, and Cornwall was still a far and remote place – quite cut off from the rest of England. But this small hotel was to play an important role in putting the little fishing village on the map.

Before the war, the local taxi driver usually met holidaymakers at the railway station in his Model T Ford and drove them to the hotel. Later, as visitors began arriving in their big, modern cars, the locals watched them negotiate the narrow streets with great amusement.

As the austere years faded into memory, the rich and famous began making their way down to Mousehole. Everything changed with the swinging '60s, when extravagance reigned and the successful made a point of enjoying their money.

Pop stars were frequent visitors to the Lobster Pot, as were the young aristocratic set. A viscount would often bring along a gaggle of titled ladies and honourables and take over a number of rooms. Huge, high-spirited dinner parties were held on the veranda. Lobster and other delicacies were tossed about, and the carpeting drank its share of champagne.

Sometimes female guests would arrive in beautiful flowing gowns, only to end up looking like moth-eaten butterflies as they dashed on stilettos from the car park in the Cornish wind and rain.

Americans also loved the Lobster Pot. The *Chicago Tribune*, which had more than 3.5 million readers, featured it as one of England's best 25 country inns.

Sylvia walks out. Mrs. Hulme in a spin.

Sometimes the staff were ill and I did the "waiting" as well as the drinks.

And sometimes Sylvia got fed up with so many people
wanting teas.

Sylvia is feeling fed up. Barbara is cheerful as always

The laundry
is having a
holiday, so
Noreen has   to do the washing

Sometimes Noreen did the washing because the laundry went on holiday.

Visits to the hotel by well-known folk from all walks of life were common. Ray Davies of the Kinks would arrive sporting a long overcoat. David Bowie was once a guest, as was Andrew Lloyd Webber. The Animals pop group turned a few heads as did actor Christopher Lee, who used to perch in a corner of the restaurant in a black cap.

Writer Daphne du Maurier travelled down from her own Cornish home. Other famous guests included singer Edmund Hockridge, actors Richard Briers and Charlton Heston, naturalist Graham Dangerfield, comedian Barry Cryer, and Pat Phoenix, who shot to fame as Elsie Tanner in the long-running television soap "Coronation Street."

On one occasion, presenter Anneka Rice raced through the hotel looking for a clue as part of the television programme "Challenge Anneka" and found it hidden under a restaurant table laden with red lobsters.

Televison cooks Fanny Craddock and her husband Johnnie spent time there. Diners described Fanny as an imposing woman whose mouth was lipsticked nearly to her nose.

Dame Judi Dench spent Christmas at the Lobster Pot in 1987, having driven down after a performance in the West End on Christmas Eve. The actress was joined by her husband, Michael Williams, daughter Finty and friends. The weather was so fine that they sat on the beach on Christmas morning. That night Dame Judi and Finty wore flashing Christmas earrings at dinner, which rather disconcerted a Japanese family at the next table. On Boxing Day, she had to commandeer a taxi to take her back to work in London.

Such was the popularity of the place that people returned year after year for their holidays – or even two or three times in the same year. The staff got to know them well and looked forward to their arrival.

The Lobster Pot became known around the world as a delightful honeymoon destination and a place to celebrate special occasions. Comedian Spike Milligan spent his second honeymoon there. And one couple travelled all the way from Heathrow Airport by taxi just to stay the night and feast on lobster specialities.

I loved going through the tiny streets of Newlyn on a bus.

Soon I became part of the harbour scene and the fishermen greeted me with their "You!" greeting.

After Cinders died, Major Kelly remarried, in 1983, and he and his new wife, Sue, continued to run the Lobster Pot for a number of years, until it ran into financial difficulties.

The lean winter months have always made Cornwall a difficult place to sustain a business. In an effort to keep money flowing during the off-season, Major Kelly started a shareholding system, but it failed. Not helped by his love of horse racing, the hotel fell into a steady decline leading to its eventual sale.

Under new ownership the hotel stayed open for a while longer. But the magic was gone, and after several erratic seasons in the late 1990's, the Lobster Pot closed its doors for the last time.

For Major Kelly, the hotel had been his life. Without it, he felt bereft.

When an American journalist came to write a story about the hotel's history, Major Kelly said that he had destroyed all the guest books and letters from both illustrious and not-so-famous guests. "You see," he later told a friend, "the Lobster Pot was my baby," then broke down and sobbed. Soon afterwards, early one morning in December 1993, he walked into the sea and drowned.

It was a sad end to a larger-than-life man who had given joy and happy memories to so many people and whose beloved hotel had played a major role in Mousehole's colourful history.

Now the building has a new life as luxury apartments, including several affordable units under the Guinness Trust. One apartment was bought by a couple from abroad who had spent many happy times at the Lobster Pot – and they now overlook Mousehole's harbour as owners, not guests.

Times move on, but for many people the world over, the Lobster Pot was someplace special from another era – a gracious small hotel in remotest West Cornwall where one Major John Kelly reigned supreme, guests were treated like royalty, and there always was a lobster in every pot.

Life is very pleasant in Mousehole, so I'm sweeping the
restaurant . . .

. . . because you might decide to come and stay at a small hotel. It's quite easy. You take a train from Paddington and go as far west as you can. You will have a warm welcome.

The beginning—

The words were by me and our office girl drew the pictures.

Daphne Radenhurst

Kate Tilley

Acknowledgements

Many thanks to **Dame Judi Dench** for taking time out from her busy filming schedule to share memories of her stay at the Lobster Pot.

Steve Ross Talbot had suggested the idea for the book at a party in Mousehole. He had longed coveted the Lobster Pot and had hoped to buy it with a business partner, a master chef in France, and return the hotel to its former glory. Alas, the venture never took off.

Eia Von Der Flur has been an enormous help – without her this little book would never have been published.

Greta Lewis, well known for her gracious entertaining, still lives near what was the former Lobster Pot. Her mother, Euphemia "Phemia" Laird, used to take in guests during the busy times. She still wears the bracelet given to her mother as a wedding memento of two hotel guests.

Hilary Warner came to work in the hotel with her family in 1959. Her mother, Phyllis McKen-Allen, was running a catering agency in London for all the big hotels including the Savoy when Major Kelly phoned saying he needed staff. Since the entire family was trained in the hotel business, they decided to come down for the season and liked it so much they never went back. Her mother was the barmaid; her father, Frederick McKen-Allen, was the manager; brother John Sharp was head waiter and sister Susan Sharp the waitress. Susan later married Major Kelly after the death of his first wife, Cinders.

Judy Sharp, who married Hilary's stepbrother, also worked at the hotel along with **Lynne Sanders**, who remembers guests going out shark fishing in "The Talisman" and bringing the catch into the harbour at night.

Janet Rowe, formerly Tregenza, worked at the Lobster Pot with her four sisters, Romola, Rachel, Caroline and Claire, her mother, Joyce, and brother-in-law Robin Richardson.

Jeanne Torrie remembers it being like a big house party when she worked there.

Pam Smith worked at the hotel for about seven years in the 1970's and described it as "an incredibly wonderful place."

Paul and Libby Harvey were regular diners at the Lobster Pot. As members of the Newlyn family business W. Harvey and Sons Shellfish Merchants, they supplied shellfish to the restaurant.

Mousehole harbourmaster **Paul Gillchrest** first moved to Cornwall with his mother, Joan, when he was 12. His grandmother used to treat him to lunch at the hotel on her visits from Maidenhead, Berkshire. Paul's wife, Jeanette, worked at the Mousehole Bird Hospital and recalls Major Kelly's generosity in sending up leftover bread to feed the birds.

Raymond Pomeroy's father was the local taxi driver and has a fund of local knowledge.

Roger Davison of Mousehole provided interesting references about Aleister Crowley's holiday.

Many thanks to **Susan Atkinson** and Nim Bawden for their photographs.

John and Lisa Peterson enjoyed wonderful summers in Mousehole and often dined on their last night at the hotel. They have gone on to buy one of the apartments.

Ray Worth like many others celebrated his engagement at the Lobster Pot.

Richard Birkhead has a painting by Betty Nankervis that he believes was hung in the hotel.

Ulf and **Margareta Larsson** holidayed there and provided a tariff card.

Heartfelt gratitude to **Melissa Hardie** of the Hypatia Trust for her encouragement, as always, and to **Angie Butler**, who is an inspiration to everyone. Above all, I thank **Donna Anton** for both her editing assistance and design of this book, which she has beautifully brought to life.

Finally, cheers to all the **staff and customers** of the dear old Lobster Pot who for so many years made it such a charming and memorable place to visit.

Kate Tilley was born in Richmond in 1912. Educated privately in Jersey, she originally wanted to be a dancer but failed the audition. Her father had put money into the famous London Windmill Theatre where she and her brother, Kenneth More, also worked. Whilst there she met and married comedian John Tilley, who was 13 years her senior. He died of cancer two years later, when Kate was only 22.

After seeking fame and fortune as a model in Hollywood and finding neither, she returned to England and remarried, but divorced after several years. She then worked as a cook-housekeeper for wealthy families, mostly abroad, in France, Spain and Bermuda.

At the invitation of film producer David Henley, whom she met at the Lobster Pot, Kate opened England's first Expresso coffee bar, in Oxford, with three businessmen who had run a restaurant with Gracie Fields in Capri. She later went to London where she worked as a salesperson and model at Harrods and Woollands and was the first model at Harrods to show off the New Look. For several years she also worked for the Freud family.

Kate now lives in a Guinness Trust home.

Daphne Radenhurst was born in France in 1928. She came to England when she was nine and won a scholarship to public school and university, where she studied modern languages.

Daphne worked in London for a few years with ICI, where she shared an office with Peggy Woodin, who had been secretary to Kate Tilley's husband in another ICI division. In 1959 Daphne went to Paris and worked for NATO, later transferring to Brussels, where she stayed for 30 years and also looked after her dependent mother. Upon retirement Daphne returned to England and received an MBE for her services to NATO. More free time allowed her to seriously take up art. She attended Bath College of Art and has had two exhibitions of her work.

Currently living in Bath, Daphne also loves to sing and go to the theatre.

Diana Ayres is a native of Cheshire and has always worked on newspapers, including *The Cornishman* in Penzance. She came to Cornwall in the swinging '60's and fell in love with its carefree lifestyle. Her first home was along Saltponds, Mousehole, in Mariners Cottage, and she walked past the Lobster Pot every day on her way to work.

After taking time out from journalism to raise her two children, Gwen and Iain, Diana saw an advertisement for a cocktail waitress at the Lobster Pot but did not apply, never dreaming that one day she would be delving into the hotel's enchanting history.

She later helped Wilmay Le Grice with her autobiography *Wilmay* and more recently co-produced *Digging for Memories: The Women's Land Army in Cornwall* for the Hypatia Trust.

Diana lives in Paul, Cornwall, with her husband, Keith. They are the proud grandparents of Kizzy and Lucy.

The Lobster Pot